SUMMARY OF
YOU
are a
BADASS:
HOW TO STOP DOUBTING YOUR GREATNESS AND START LIVING AN AWESOME LIFE

**Proudly Brought To You By
BOOK ADDICT**

WITH KEY POINTS
&
KEY TAKE AWAY

Copyright © 2018; By BOOK ADDICT.

All rights reserved. No part of this publication may be reproduced, distributed, or transmitted in any form or by any means, including photocopying, recording, or other electronic or mechanical methods, without the prior written permission of the publisher, except in the case of brief quotations embodied in critical reviews and certain other noncommercial uses permitted by copyright law.

Disclaimer

This book is a summary and meant to be a great companionship to the original book or to simply help you get the gist of the original book. If you're looking for the original book, kindly go to Amazon website, and search for You Are a Badass by Jen Sincero.

Table of Contents

EXECUTIVE SUMMARY 6
CHAPTER 1: MY SUBCONSCIOUS MADE ME DO IT 8
    Key Takeaways: 8
CHAPTER 2: THE G WORD 15
    Key Takeaways: 15
CHAPTER 3: PRESENT AS A PIGEON 21
    Key Takeaways: 21
CHAPTER 4: THE BIG SNOOZE 25
    Key Takeaways: 25
CHAPTER 5: SELF-PERCEPTION IS A ZOO 29
    Key Takeaways: 29
CHAPTER 6: LOVE THE ONE YOU IS 32
    Key Takeaways: 32
CHAPTER 7: I KNOW YOU ARE BUT WHAT AM I? 36
    Key Takeaways: 36
CHAPTER 8: WHAT ARE YOU DOING HERE? 39
    Key Takeaways: 39
CHAPTER 9: LOINCLOTH MAN 41
    Key Takeaways: 41
CHAPTER 10: MEDITATION 101 42
    Key Takeaways: 42
CHAPTER 11: YOUR BRAIN IS YOUR BITCH 45
    Key Takeaways: 45
Chapter 12: LEAD WITH YOUR CROTCH 47

 Key Takeaways: 47

Chapter 13: GIVE AND LET GIVE 49

 Key Takeaways: 49

Chapter 14: GRATITUDE: THE GATEWAY DRUG TO AWESOMENESS 51

 Key Takeaways: 51

Chapter 15: FORGIVE OR FESTER 53

 Key Takeaways: 53

Chapter 16: LOOSEN YOUR BONE, WILMA 56

 Key Takeaways: 56

Chapter 17: IT'S SO EASY ONCE YOU FIGURE OUT IT ISN'T HARD 57

 Key Takeaways: 57

Chapter 18: PROCRASTINATION, PERFECTION, AND A POLISH BEER GARDEN 60

 Key Takeaways: 60

Chapter 19: THE DRAMA OF OVERWHELM 62

 Key Takeaways: 62

Chapter 20: FEAR IS FOR SUCKERS 65

 Key Takeaways: 65

Chapter 21: MILLIONS OF MIRRORS 67

 Key Takeaways: 67

Chapter 22: THE SWEET LIFE 70

 Key Takeaways: 70

Chapter 23: THE ALMIGHTY DECISION 71

 Key Takeaways: 71

Chapter 24: MONEY, YOUR NEW BEST FRIEND 73
    Key Takeaways: 73
Chapter 25: REMEMBER TO SURRENDER 76
    Key Takeaways: 76
Chapter 26: DOING VS. SPEWING 78
    Key Takeaways: 78
Chapter 27: BEAM ME UP, SCOTTY 80
    Key Takeaways: 80

EXECUTIVE SUMMARY

Jen Sincero's book *"You Are a Badass: How to Stop Doubting Your Greatness and Start Living an Awesome Life"* is a guide on how to live your best life. Whether your life totally sucks at the moment, or you're living averagely and know you have untapped potential, this book is for you.

Sincero writes from experience as a woman whose life once sucked and as a professional coach helping people whose lives suck. She recognizes the high level of skepticism directed at self-help topics, yet she ventures the terrain with detailed explanations and many personal stories.

This book addresses how human beings come about their unfulfilling lives, explaining how the subconscious- which is often overlooked- in fact plays a vital role. According to Sincero, no true improvement can be made unless we acknowledge and establish a connection with Source Energy.

She also addresses other areas that are essential to the Improvement journey. A few of those include fear, faith, forgiveness, negative thoughts, meditation, and many more. She provides practical tips on dealing with each of these issues.

Sincero's main themes are simple:

- You are an awesome individual with so much potential.
- All you need and all you'll ever be is in existence already and you need to be connected to Source Energy to access them.

Her book teaches you how to do just that.

CHAPTER 1: MY SUBCONSCIOUS MADE ME DO IT

Key Takeaways:
- *The conscious mind takes longer to mature than the subconscious mind*
- *Our subconscious is in the driver's seat. Most of our realities today are shaped and directed by the subliminal.*
- *We experience internal conflict when our conscious, intentional mind wants something, and our subconscious wants the opposite.*
- *The first step to overcoming the subconscious is becoming aware and acknowledging its huge influence on your life.*

Years back, I had a very painful experience, literally. On a particular bowling expedition with my friends, I slipped and ended up crashing my butt on the extremely hard floor. Waking up in the middle of the night as a result of agonizing pain in my feet became a norm and I was told I'd need a stronger mattress if I ever intended to have a good night's sleep.

Shopping for a new mattress was awkward, but it was worse when I had to blurt out my frustrations to the mattress guy who chose to lie beside me as I tried out the merchandise. After debating a couple of options in my head, I decided to slip out of the store without my mattress guy noticing. I thought of asking him to get off; letting him know he was making me uncomfortable. I thought of requesting another salesperson to attend to me. But I didn't do any of these things. I was too much of my parents' daughter.

I grew up in a home where it was the practice to avoid awkward situations. Instead of clearing things up, we'd act like it never happened and talk about something completely irrelevant instead. My mother was raised by rigid parents and even though she tried her best not to give us the kind of home she grew up in, she somehow couldn't pass on a healthy approach to confrontation. Most of the time, you're not to blame for the messed-up traits you have or the situation you initially find yourself in. Often times, these can be traced to your upbringing and childhood experiences. But when you *remain* that way, now the blame is yours.

At birth, you were an innocent creature, oblivious of the trappings that made the world complicated. You had no idea you were supposed to wear clothes, much less an obsession over designer labels and what not. You just existed. Then, as you grew and discovered more of your world, you came in contact with folks who gave you the supposed 'blueprint'. They told you the things to be done and those that couldn't be done. They basically gave you a bunch of life Dos and Don'ts, and consciously or subconsciously, you find yourself inculcating those values. You find your life playing out in line with said values.

We all know the first and foremost culprits of this blueprint creators, don't we? Yes, it's your parents. The bigger world chips in sooner or later as well, but it is at home that you get your first lessons. Often times, parents mean well. They don't go out intending to hurt you. In fact, they tell you most of the things they do out of love and concern for their child, who they also see as their responsibility. In the process, some of these life principles they're passing on are not originally theirs. So, at the end of the day, you're getting their principles and the principles of their own parents, and the parents before that and the ones before that. We need to free ourselves from the untruths we have followed from one generation to another.

Every human being has a conscious and a subconscious. The conscious parts of our mind, also called the frontal lobe, is the active fellow; making sense of things, analyzing, administering, deciding, etc. Our conscious mind is only at rest when we're asleep and it reaches the stage of maturity around the same time as the onset of puberty. Our subconscious, on the other hand comes fully developed, and we come into it right from the day we are born. Unlike the conscious, this part of us is totally not into any form of scrutiny or evaluation. It is from this part that feelings, emotions, irrational behavior, etc. Emanate. When we're born, knowing nothing and exploring our world for the first time, all those dos and don'ts we get from folks around us are stowed in the subconscious.

As you may guess, this is the part of our minds that allow basically anything to pass through our filter of acceptance. This is why, as children, we didn't find it ridiculous to believe that there was a Santa or that people in our family just didn't become rich ever.

Most of the problems we find with ourselves today can be traced to certain faulty subconscious principles that have held us bound. If we are to break free from so many of our limitations, we must demystify the topic of the subconscious. Basically:

- The map and directions for our lives reside in the subconscious. They consist of everything we've being told about life as kids; the dos and don'ts.
- Most of the time, we remain unaware of these subliminal principles and their huge effect on our lives.
- Our conscious minds, no matter how logical and intelligent, remain largely subordinate to our subconscious. Interesting, isn't it? Remember, the subconscious if fully formed at birth while the conscious mind still has a long way before it reaches that.

So don't be too surprised when it turns out you're acting out everything your conscious mind suggests but you're still finding it difficult to break free from limitations and live your best life. A child raised by a deadbeat dad who also fails to care for his kid may end up taking a few things into her subconscious.

For instance, her subconscious may convince her to equate money with hard, unproductive work, or she may grow a resentment for money because it kept her father from being there for her. That same child, now grown, may find that no matter how much she intentionally wants to make money, she always ends up making money and losing it because she thinks it will get her abandoned by a loved one. The last thing we usually think of, when we're failing in our quest to live the excellent life, is that our subconscious mind is in the driver's seat. So often times we want the best life- we want to live to our full potential- but our subconscious is dictating an opposite path. Conflict ensues and we're stuck in a rut. We want something but we're tilting towards something else.

If you're going to break free from the hold of subconscious values, then the first thing to do is to acknowledge their existence. If you have no idea what you're dealing with, you're never going to face it squarely. You'll keep making the wrong moves- making conscious efforts to overcome subconscious challenges- and getting the wrong results. If you're finding it impossible to make money, or just having money problems generally, do a simple exercise. Write down the thoughts that pop into your head when you think about money. Evaluate what you have written and determine whether those thoughts are more negative or positive. Evaluate your parents' principles concerning money, or the principles of the folks you grew up with, and see how it tallies with yours.

This book contains a lot of tools that will help you navigate the course of overcoming those limiting subconscious beliefs. Your first step however, should be an active mindfulness of the subconscious mind and its important role in your life. You need to assess those areas where you need help and identify which subconscious belief is at work. It is only then that you can start clearing out the bad stuff and making way for new, enabling principles that will guide you to your best life.

CHAPTER 2: THE G WORD

Key Takeaways:
- *Keep an open mind about the concept of God and spirituality*
- *God is very central to the life-improvement journey you seek to embark upon*
- *You can call it whatever you want, as long as you recognize & keep a relationship with the Energy that powers your being*
- *Your essence gives off vibrations, & so does every other thing you want or don't want*
- *Your vibrations must be on the same frequency as that of the things you desire*
- *You must take determined, definite steps towards seeing the manifestation of your desires*
- *Your faith must outweigh every fear*

Sometime ago, me and my friends would regularly chill at a particular bar in New Mexico. Our constant visits were not as a result of how much we liked hanging out there per se. It was because the bar was so Western and we were so Eastern. We had fun laughing at cowboys- their distinct clothes and moustaches- and watched awestruck as the regulars did the line dancing effortlessly. We were a bunch of snobbish East Coast folks looking down our noses at the Westerners. While still poking fun at the dance, we would join in sometimes and not care about our mismatched steps. But each day we joined in, we learnt a little bit more of the routine, and eventually we were really good at the dance. We were not just good at it though. We were enjoying it! Soon enough, we weren't going to the bar because we wanted to poke fun at anyone. We were going because we genuinely and excitedly looked forward to dancing like we had no cares in the world.

This is a perfect depiction of how my journey with God panned out. I had always been highly skeptical of anything that to do with "God"; just hearing the word was a turn-off. But I was at such a low place in my life that I was willing to try anything, anyone that could help me get up. I was penniless and my life looked like it was headed for an unknown destination because I wasn't sure what it was about anymore. I guess my situation changed my perspective, because this time, when I came across anything God-related in the numerous self-help books I was consuming, I wasn't so cynical anymore.

I actually wanted to give the many pieces of spiritual advice a try. And what do you know, it wasn't bad at all! I gave it another try, and another, until I was constantly applying it in my life. It was a case of mind transformation. Before long, I was feeling better and being better. At this point, I was largely trusting of the God/spirituality route and applied it to every aspect of my life. I was hooked, seeing something I once despised transform my life so radically and positively. I could not keep something so phenomenal to myself and I started telling others about it; teaching them how to work with it.

Now, I know people have varying opinions on this issue; it's definitely one of the most controversial topics in the world. Regardless of where you belong on that opinion spectrum, you'll need to stay receptive to whatever you might come to learn to at least contemplate the idea if you're serious about transforming your life positively. You need to be able to consider it instead of shutting your ears and minds the minute you hear 'God'. There are a bunch of names out there that different people choose to call God. That doesn't matter at all. As a personal preference, I prefer using names like The Spirit, The Universe, Source Energy, or The Vortex, but as long as you know the source of the energy radiating operating within you; the force that drives your existence.

As long as you cultivate a consciousness of and relationship with that energy, you can call it whatever you're comfortable with. It is this force that propels us- if we let it- throughout the duration of our lives, helping us grow as we navigate. Finding out that there was more to me than literally meets the eye was quite enlightening and I was propelled to dig deeper into this realm of the spiritual. The fact that I wrote this book is evidence enough that I found that decision rewarding.

Connecting with my Source Energy gives me an unusual clarity of the physical realm, and at the same time unites me with a spiritual realm. I feel genuine happiness flowing through my being and I am empowered to achieve all the things I set out to achieve. Establishing all I want for my life becomes effortless and I am truly at peace. Since I fell in love with my Source Energy, I've never had cause to regret.

Every adjustment you'll be making in your life is hinged on these three things:

- The cosmos consists of Source Energy
- Every force operates at a certain frequency. You pulsate at a certain level. Your aspirations pulsate at a certain frequency. Those things you want to do away with also vibrate at a certain frequency.
- One vibration frequency attracts similar vibration frequencies.

So basically, what you invest your attention in is what you attract to yourself. If you're vibrating at a low frequency, dwelling on negative feelings such as pessimism, jealousy, worry, shame, etc. you cannot attract vibrations with high frequencies (positive outcomes). Whatever frequency you're disseminating should correspond with the vibration frequency of what you're looking to attract. Once you can achieve this, you'll be amazed at how things just appear to fall in place for you. That's because you're sending out high frequency vibrations, your Source Energy takes note, and you attract people and things with similar frequencies.

Everything you want your life to be is within reach. The abundance of prospects and experiences can be easily accessed once you can give off energy corresponding to that of your desires and be determined about improving your life. Yes, you have to be downright resolute on this quest because, contrary to what many people assume, this is not all about thinking high frequency and feeling good. This journey requires you to put in the work as well, and not all of it will be enjoyable. When you're consciously giving off the right vibes and doing the right things, you'll see incredible results.

Doing the right things without the right kind of energy will create a situation in which there is no effortless flow. You'll struggle too much while trying to achieve what you ordinarily shouldn't break a sweat over, and even then, you can only get lucky to actually succeed. The only way to be sure of success is to have a well-defined list of what you genuinely desire, have the conviction that those things are within reach irrespective of where you are at the moment, remain in touch with Source Energy, maintain the highest frequency you can, and put in calculated, determined work. It's a tested and trusted recipe!

Your convictions play a major role in how your life turns out. You must continue to believe that something is possible if you want to achieve it. Your faith must remain unshaken, even when it seems unreasonable. Once you lose faith, the universe recognizes that, and you'll stop attracting the right kind of things to yourself. Holding on to this faith can be daunting. It means- regardless of what surrounds you- believing the best; those positives you want for your life. It means uplifting your faith above any fear whatsoever.

CHAPTER 3: PRESENT AS A PIGEON

Key Takeaways:
- *We often find it impossible to bask in the simplicity of the present*
- *The Universe sometimes jolts us to awareness of the present*
- *Animals & Children are great examples*
- *Dwelling on the past or obsessing over the future leads us to giving off low frequency vibrations and attracting people & things with the same*

One of the things that fill me with dread the most in Yoga class is hearing the instructor ask us to do the Pigeon Pose. Let's just say it's not the easiest pose in Yoga. I was always freaking out because I was so sure I would get stuck while trying to achieve the pose. So on this particular day when my Yoga instructor asked for the Pigeon Pose, my reaction was no different. While he was giving a lecture on our bond with The Universe and our pathway to illumination, my thoughts were scattered everywhere, mostly fear-based.

I thought of all the things that could go wrong while I was in that pose, but something else happened. I suddenly let go. I took a deep breath, stopped my panicking, muted the fearful voices in my head, and fell in rhythm with the Pigeon Pose. Next thing I know, I'm actually doing the Pose! I go way past the point I've ever gone before and I don't feel an ounce of pain. I can feel myself approaching a higher realm, but before I get there, I suddenly think I'm stuck and all the initial fears come rushing back. Then I silence the fears again and reconnect with the Pigeon Pose.

This depicts how many of us act out our lives. One minute we're basking in the serenity of the present, the next, we're losing our heads over a million and one fears. I often wonder at how common it is to see people worry about who likes them, how much hair is growing on their face, why the internet is so slow! We constantly lose our peace when we should be soaking up the present. Our universe is filled with so many things that we should be excited about and grateful for- water, air, kindness, music, flowers, love- yet we're fixated on the inconsequential. Sometimes The Universe jolts our awareness of the wonders surrounding us. Close brushes with death usually do the trick. Seeing how close you are to losing it all gives you an appreciation of the many joys you've ignored for so long. All the fuss you made about so many things will suddenly not matter anymore, and just the fact that you're breathing becomes such an experience.

The Universe has also strategically provided us with cues. Animals and children are two of the most in-the-moment creatures. Notice how kids are always engrossed in whatever they're doing at every moment. They are not encumbered by thoughts of how not to play, who not to play with, and other similar thoughts that burden adults.

Everything you want and more is already in existence. That may sound weird, but consider electricity. It has always been, but not until the light bulb did we become really aware of it. So also, everything with which we want to enhance our lives is already available. We only need to access it by remaining present in the Now and connecting to Source Energy. Recognize and enjoy what is happening- breathing, seeing, living. Be aware of the delight and tranquility present in the moment.

I know that as adults, you probably have huge responsibilities. Yes, you should think of the future and make plans towards it. You should think of the past to gather lessons for the future, or to encourage yourself for the journey ahead. Whatever the case, whether you're visiting the future or the past, remember not to linger. Therein lies our problem. We often linger and allow negative thoughts to creep in and distort our positive energy.

On the other hand, being in the moment mutes the fearful noises in your head, thereby making it easier for you to be in sync with Source Energy. This places your vibrations at a high frequency and you can attract similar high-frequency people, things, and experiences.

CHAPTER 4: THE BIG SNOOZE

Key Takeaways:
- *The Ego wants to preserve false, limiting principles that your subconscious imbibed a long time ago*
- *Attempting to get rid of the Ego attracts opposition from it*
- *Don't be shocked if your loved ones kick at your decision to transform your life*
- *Surround yourself with people of high frequency*
- *To see the manifestation of your improved life, you'll have to keep moving in spite of the chaos Ego throws at you*

One constantly misunderstood concept is the Ego. What typically comes to mind is a sense of superiority and pride; that thing that makes people so obsessed with themselves and gives them a sense of importance over everybody else. I used to think this too, until I began to explore the world of self-help. Then I got to realize that the Ego is not some abstract concept existing outside the human being. Ego is a person's doppelganger; the other self that takes charge on many occasions. Ego is also not a one-way street, which means it can be expressed in various ways. For instance, a woman that repeatedly turns down opportunities to take up her dream of acting simply because somewhere in her subconscious, she's terrified of having people meet her true person. That's Ego at work. A man that won't stop talking about how awesome and so much better his life is than any other's because of deep insecurities and an innate need to be validated by other people. That's the Ego acting out.

I call Ego the Big Snooze- BS- because being unaware of how much power and wonder The Universe carries is the main reason why we still live messed-up lives. The BS is powered by those untruths that have been programmed into your subconscious from birth; those principles that limit you and lead you to make decisions that are not healthy or pleasing for you. The BS is also hung up on what other people think about you and goes through life acting as the injured party. It works with fear to keep you firmly within the limits of those untrue principles you've imbibed all those years, and it promotes the idea that you are disconnected from everything else in the universe.

Your genuine self however, is the exact opposite. It feeds off your connection with Source Energy, validates internally, takes charge of life, works with love instead of fear, and explores the endless limits of The Universe. Your genuine self exists in the present and accepts that you are united with a Universe that is filled with wonder. Usually, we all have BS times and non-BS times. Unfortunately, too many of us stay too long in the BS periods, settling for a life that sucks at pretty much everything. We refuse to tap into the abundance laid out before us by The Universe and stick with the untruths that continually limit us.

So many are not even aware that they can break free from the BS zone because our society is largely discouraging of people who are pushing beyond the limits and getting their best lives. Don't be surprised if your loved ones are the first to give you a stern lecture when you decide to venture out of your comfort zone. Most times, these people do it out of love, but them rehashing your fears only does more harm than good. For your own good, avoid arguing with them or being around them. Surround yourself with like minds; people giving off high-frequency vibrations like yourself.

Truth is, the Big Snooze doesn't want you venturing outside the familiar, comfy zone, so it's going to put up a fight when you try to do that and make something out of your life. Think of smoking or drug addiction and the horrible withdrawal symptoms that follow when you quit. That is the BS revolting at your move towards improvement. Don't quit or be discouraged because that is exactly what the BS is trying to achieve. When you receive all those hard knocks while you're trying to improve your life, just remember it is a sign that you're on course and working towards eliminating the BS.

CHAPTER 5: SELF-PERCEPTION IS A ZOO

Key Takeaways:
- *It's natural to have occasional feelings of self-doubt but you mustn't let them linger*
- *See yourself from the eyes of the outsider and it'll be easier to acknowledge your brilliance*
- *Doubting yourself and believing you're a total badass take the same level of energy*
- *You have a distinct purpose in the Universe's grand scheme of things. You are cherished.*

One of the most fascinating women I know is also a certified speaker, yet she sometimes thinks her talks are uninteresting. She's not alone in this phenomenon. I also know a couple of other brilliant people killing it in their various fields, who experience constant bouts of self-doubt and incompetence. And we're all usually like this. One minute we see and accept how awesome we are, the next we're afraid that not only are we incompetent, but that very soon the whole world will notice. We beat ourselves up with negative perceptions, wasting energy that could as well be expended on accepting our charm and brilliance.

Interestingly, we find it easy to acknowledge that someone we know did something so phenomenal. We believe in the awesomeness of that person, yet find it difficult to do the same for ourselves. Our self-perception is mostly unflattering compared to how we see other people. So maybe we all need to see ourselves from the eyes of the outsider; the outsider who believes in us and knows that we're all shades of awesome. We need to view ourselves out of our own selves, to see the radiance inside.

It's completely up to you to decide how you define your reality; how you perceive your circumstances. If you have so much power, why would you choose to spend it visualizing yourself as anything less than the awesome creature you are? Whether you like it or not, you serve an irreplaceable purpose in the Universe's grand scheme of things. You're completely amazing and that's that!

You are cherished. You are flawless. You are a masterpiece. The Universe does not want you to see yourself less than you are. It wants you to live in the awareness of your strength and true qualities. It wants you to do away with thoughts of low-frequency and know that you have limitless possibilities. It wants you to accept everything about you *(yes, even those things you think are downsides)* as a part of the perfect you. It wants you to be happy, love yourself and others, and know that you can change anything and be anything.

CHAPTER 6: LOVE THE ONE YOU IS

Key Takeaways:
- *We spend way too much time and energy convincing ourselves that we don't measure up.*
- *Loving yourself is not arrogance. It is genuine recognition of your awesomeness and healthy acceptance of your flaws.*
- *Until you can genuinely love yourself, your life will not improve.*

I once watched my 2-year old nephew as he bent to pick things off the floor. Unlike most adults, he bent at the knees, not his lower back. At birth, we have an intuitive comprehension of pretty much every life basics. We have faith in our impulses. We eat when hunger strikes, we love, we laugh, we cry without caring how we look or what anyone thinks about it. Then as we grow, we interact with other people and we pick up fallacious, negative beliefs. Our subconscious is fed this poison and our lives begin to pattern after the same. This leads to agony- physical and emotional- and we can choose how to respond.

We may decide to drown our pain with food, alcohol, or drugs.

We may decide to resign to a life of mediocrity.

We may decide to acknowledge our *badassness* and exit the rut.

We have all these resources at our disposal, to be the best of ourselves. Yet, we spend them most in convincing ourselves that we don't measure up. We come into the world as free spirits, loving ourselves completely. Yet, as we navigate through the world and gather experiences, we gradually lose that love. Loving yourself is not arrogance. It is genuine recognition of your awesomeness and healthy acceptance of your flaws. You realize that you're allowed to make mistakes and easily forgive yourself, not hoarding resentment or guilt. Our world would be a much better place if everyone could genuinely love themselves and not be intimidated by what someone else thinks.

To reach this happy place, you must:

- Recognize and truly understand how exceptional you are. There is no one- *absolutely no one!* - like you in The Universe and your place cannot be filled by anyone else.
- Immerse yourself in positive declarations of what you want your life to be. Don't just say them though.

Believe them, no matter how corny or unreasonable they sound.

- Take time to do those things that truly make you happy, and don't feel selfish about it. If you've been putting off something you love for so long, do it now! Be happy. Put yourself first and look out for you.
- Identify and be sensitive to the areas where you beat yourself up with negative thoughts. Then, replace those thoughts with more constructive, less criticizing thoughts, and take decisive action when you need to.
- Stop it with the negative jokes you make about yourself because the more you speak it, the more you become it.
- Stop responding negatively to positive comments about yourself. Accept compliments sincerely.
- Pay attention to your body's needs- baths, clean clothes, exercise, sex, you name it! You'll be a happier, more productive person if your body feels good.
- Stop the comparison game and genuinely celebrate your accomplishments. You're not in a race with anyone because your path is unique.

- Cultivate the ability to forgive yourself of all the messed-up things you've done in the past, and even the ones you'll still do. Messing up is human. Give yourself a break.
- Fall in love… with yourself.

CHAPTER 7: I KNOW YOU ARE BUT WHAT AM I?

Key Takeaways:

- *Stop obsessing over people's reactions to you. You have no control over it anyway.*
- *Nobody who lived their best life ever cared what other people said.*
- *Take every criticism or commendation and weigh it against the truth.*

Sometime in the past, my friend, who is a placed a frightful call across to me. As it turned out, she was freaking out because she thought the book she was currently working on would make people think of her as a creepy person. Now here's something you need to learn, just in case you haven't:

If you're ever gonna be the best of you, you will have to stop giving a rat's ass what people think of you.

For most of us, our teenage and young adult years were spent obsessing over what people would think or say. We said and did stuff based on this. For some of us, that way of life fizzled out as we grew. Sadly, many of us still remain fixated on patterning our lives after other people's opinions. So let's say you're about to make a choice or decide between an Option A and Option B, there are only 3 things you need to concern yourself with. Actually, they're more like questions. Whatever it is you want to do, ask yourself:

- Do I want to be this thing? Do I want to do this thing? Do I want to have this thing?
- Does this decision constitute a step towards where I *WANT* to go?
- Will anybody be harmed as a result of this step I intend to take?

It's easy to give two cents about what other people will think or say about us, but hey, look around, nobody who accomplished something huge or lived their best life ever let what other people think stop them. No, they forged ahead regardless of any dissenting voice. You'll hear the dissenting voices too, once you decide and take a step out of the 'normal'. But here's something to remember as well:

You have no control over people's reactions to your decisions anyway.

So whether you're obsessed with how people will condemn your action or how they proclaim you're the best thing since sliced bread, you're on the wrong path. You can't build your self-esteem on what other people say because then, when they suddenly decide to think and say otherwise (and they do have power over that, remember?), you may find yourself at a loss to define who you are.

To rid yourself of this obsession, you will need to:

- Question the motive behind every of your actions. See if external opinion is behind that action or whether it is of freewill and integrity.
- Give your 100% to everything you do. It makes it more unlikely that you'll be moved by what someone else has to say about it.
- Learn to develop conviction in your instincts and hone your connectedness with Source Energy.
- Follow the example of a role model. This is only for the meantime while you're trying to learn how not to care about other people's reactions.
- Be in love with yourself.

Now, all these do not mean you should completely shut your ears to other people's opinions. Sometimes, people can see in us what we do not see in ourselves, so their opinions can come in handy. Whether it is a condemnation or a commendation from other people, take the time to search within yourself if this opinion reflects the truth. If so, aim to use it to improve your life and that of others. If it turns out to be false, leave it be and move on with your life.

CHAPTER 8: WHAT ARE YOU DOING HERE?

Key Takeaways:
- *Until you discover that purpose and start giving, you have not truly begun living.*
- *Go after your dreams, no matter how weird they seem.*
- *Pay attention to your instincts.*

We all know that great feeling that comes with giving someone a gift; the excitement that surrounds that moment as you watch your gift being unwrapped by the receiver. That is exactly how it is when you've identified your gift to the world; the purpose for which you were born. This is also why you feel adrift when you're yet to discover that purpose. Until you discover that purpose and start *giving*, you have not truly begun living. This may sound difficult to you. You may be wondering why you're yet to discover this unique purpose of yours. Worry not, you do have a purpose, and it is only waiting for you to discover it.

So how do you find out what this gift of yours is, and how do you go about giving it to the world?

- Audit your life through the eyes of an alien. Sometimes, over-familiarity with yourself blinds you to your gifts.
- Do something! Free yourself from the trap of wasting time, over-analyzing and pitching one idea against another and seeing which is perfect.
- Be first-class at whatever you're doing at the moment. Even though your present engagement may not be your calling, it is a part of your journey towards that calling.
- Take a cue from what you find so fascinating in other people's lives.
- Don't be stuck on the idea that your gift must be one grand idea that will be revealed in an exceptional flash of discernment. Your calling may as well be two or more things. Keep an open mind.
- Be attentive to your instincts.
- Go after your dreams, no matter how weird they seem.
- Adore yourself.

CHAPTER 9: LOINCLOTH MAN

Key Takeaways:
- *Be in love with you, regardless of who you actually are*
- *Take pleasure in the moment and embrace your person*

I once had the opportunity of meeting a very unusual man. My friends and I had gone hiking as usual when we came across him in one of the remotest mountains ever. He was a young, good-looking man with only a piece of cloth tied at the waist for clothing. He told us how he lived in a rock and only ate what nature provided, he also only used what nature provided, which was why his bed was the hide of a deer he had skinned himself. But his weirdness was not what struck me the most. It was his unabashed demeanor. Here was a man who was comfortable in his own skin and did not care about how different his chosen path was different from the majority.

That day, I envied the man his freedom.

Be in love with you, regardless of who you actually are.

CHAPTER 10: MEDITATION 101

Key Takeaways:

- *Meditation is not just sitting in one place. It means establishing a connection with Source Energy*
- *Use guided meditation if you're new at meditation*
- *Meditation increases your frequency and empowers you to receive the limitless resources in the Universe*

Meditation is another commonly misunderstood self-help concept. People think it is simply about sitting in one spot, doing nothing, but it is more. There's usually a lot rolling around in our brains, and sadly most of it are insignificant to our lives. You meditate to mute all the noise in your head and establish a connection with Source Energy. Before going into meditation proper, you might want to take this tip:

Start with about 5 to 10 minutes every day and work your way up

Don't be distracted with a bunch of rules about where and when to meditate, or whatever other complications you come across. The most important thing is that you do it. The more you do, the more you strengthen your connection with Source Energy. Among other things, the benefits of that connection include:

- Improving your instinctiveness and capacity to keep focus
- Increasing your frequency
- Stress relief
- Making you receptive to the limitless info and knowledge in the Universe
- Permeating your person with love and illumination
- Conveying you into the now
- Relaxation
- Maintaining a bright mood
- Empowerment to love yourself
- Enabling you be in tune with your inner voice

So how does this meditation thing work? Try these:

- Sit cross-legged and place our hands in your laps or on your knees.
- Maintain a relaxed posture. Loosen your forehead and jaw
- You can keep your eyes open or shut, whichever suits you.
- Concentrate on your breathing. Pay attention to it as it moves in and out of you.
- Thoughts will stray into your head. Discard them and get back to concentrating on your breathing. Also

tune in to your instinctive voice for any insights. It's not a rule though, so if nothing comes, don't freak out. Just keep repeating the process.

You may also find a couple of tips useful, such as lighting a candle and staring at it for concentration or chanting a familiar yet neutral word when the thoughts in your head are particularly active.

Guided meditation is a good idea too, especially if you're new at meditation and still have trouble curbing your scattered thoughts. You can either get meditation DVDs or visit centers where guided meditation is carried out.

CHAPTER 11: YOUR BRAIN IS YOUR BITCH

Key Takeaways:
- *The thoughts you dwell on are those you feed and they will define your reality*
- *Direct your brain to think the right thoughts*
- *Let your actions correspond with your thoughts*

Not many of us pause and think about what a mastermind the Universe must be. No, all you see today did not just happen. They were conceived and constructed, and we are now a part of this intricate collection. More than that, man is the intelligence with which man was designed. So you see why positive thoughts and meditation are essential to improvement of your life? Your thoughts carry immense power! With your thoughts, you paint the image of your future and even if right now, you're living beyond your potential, you can take the first step towards changing that by changing your thoughts accordingly.

You may find it difficult to reconcile your present 'sucks-as-hell' life with the future you in your head. You're probably not comfortable with calling that future image the truth when your present is so glaringly opposite. Well, that is exactly how it works. The thoughts you think and dwell upon are the thoughts you give life to, so feed the right thoughts. The emphasis here is on faith, the kind that will get you a lot of criticism, but if you're going to improve your life, you need to show the Universe how serious you are by directing your brain.

So how can this be done?

- Make your request known explicitly. Put it out in the Universe that you want this or that, believe you have it, and wait to see it realized.
- Let your belief be backed by actions. Take steps in faith towards the fulfillment of your dreams.
- Find ways to make your present conditions better. Surround yourself with people and things that show the Universe you're ready for improvement.
- Have a vision board with pictorial representations of where you see yourself. Images have a way of influencing our senses much more than words do.
- Roll with the right crowd; folks who already think and act the way you look forward to thinking and acting.
- Be in love with yourself. Always.

Chapter 12: LEAD WITH YOUR CROTCH

Key Takeaways:
- *Always tune in to that little child in you who was carefree and creative*
- *Maintain a positive outlook to life*
- *Don't get so "old" that you forget to be young and have fun*

Youths have the ability to brainstorm, come up with amazing ideas and execute them without really "counting the cost" because they haven't encountered too many disappointments and believe that they aren't going to lose their lives just yet. Youths venture into many risky things without really thinking of the penalties. However, with that same outlook to life, they also come up with brilliant and fancy ideas and execute them nicely.

The issue comes when people grow up because they believe that being free-spirited and creative is only for the young and facing responsibilities that come with being grown up is the sole thing they do. It's not about being reckless and foolish but it's about fulfilling your dreams and ambitions no matter what rung of the ladder called life that you are. Do not settle for the average just because you are getting "old". No matter your age, you have a right to aspire and your aspirations are yours but you have to deliberately learn to leave all your negative experiences behind.

Concentrate on positive things that life has to offer and de-emphasize the collection of negatives you have gathered all through your life. Maintain that positive outlook no matter what life throws at you. A method of achieving this is by tapping into that childish innocence when you had no absolute care in the world. It sounds weird but it works.

There are a few points of insight below:

- Approach life with a bad-ass attitude. Live life with a "why-not" mindset not critically waiting for the "perfect" time which may never come.
- Do things that make you lose yourself so much so that you don't realize the long hours you've spent on them.
- Don't lose the novice side to you. Take what you're doing seriously, rehearse as much as you need to, build yourself, keep getting better but don't lose the spark and interest you had when you were an amateur.
- Make sure you love yourself.

Chapter 13: GIVE AND LET GIVE

Key Takeaways:
- *Giving sets you in a position to receiving*
- *Giving is aligning yourself with the Universe*

Giving birth is a euphoric feeling. It is a deep gesture because it proves that you believe that there is surplus in the world so you can give out of the one you have. It also builds your faith and positions you in the giving cycle in a way that you are able to receive. Being afraid that there is not enough or that more is coming encourages you to tightly cling to the one you have which further emphasizes and strengthens the exact thing you are running away from which is insufficiency.

Life has many parallels; there are actions which birth reactions so it does not work when we try to alter natural courses; life is give and take. Obtaining is panic-based but giving away is aligning with the natural cycle. If you want to feel good and happy, learn to give happiness.

There are some ways to align yourself in the giving cycle: donate to a cause often till it becomes a habit, give something you love very much to someone who would value it, tip double what you usually tip, be nice to someone to who is nasty to you, say kinds word people and make them laugh, indulge people so as to give them the opportunity to give to you, pause and check how elated you feel being in the cycle and increase your giving level and then finally, love yourself.

Chapter 14: GRATITUDE: THE GATEWAY DRUG TO AWESOMENESS

Key Takeaways:
- *Be grateful for things you have now and the ones you aspire for*
- *When you are grateful, you have positive energy which will attract positive things to you*
- *Find the good in the bad circumstances*

Being grateful is not limited to being polite. People can be mannered and polite even if they don't feel that way, but being grateful is having a heartfelt gratitude for the little things that have gone the way you want them to. When you appreciate someone deeply for doing something for you, you feel good and the person you are thanking also feels good. That way, you have good vibes and you have higher tendencies to attract good and positive things.

On the other hand, when someone gets on your nerves or pisses you off, you attract negative vibes and you have lower tendencies to give off positive vibes. When you are in the state of gratitude, you appreciate someone and then the positive vibes you have given off bounces back to you. It is similar to the feeling you get when someone is laughing at something you said.

Being grateful helps build your faith. Faith is what you rely on when you decide to reach out into the unknown and do something which wasn't realizable in your present situation. When you are grateful, you know that there is an abundant supply of awesomeness so you can reach out and do something new, something you really do not know the outcome of.

Furthermore, you have to also be grateful for those amazing things that are coming in advance. So it's not enough to have faith that they will come but you have to also be grateful even when they have not yet arrived. There are ways to do this below:

- Always find the good thing in whatever happens to you, whether good, bad or ugly. Doing this makes it easier for you to be grateful no matter the situation.
- Before you retire for the night, do a daily review of all the things you are thankful for ranging from the big obvious ones to the minute small ones. In plain terms, count your blessings.
- Again, love yourself. Show gratitude for how far you've come and how far you're going.

Chapter 15: FORGIVE OR FESTER

Key Takeaways:
- *When you hold a grudge against someone, you have handed your happiness over to them*
- *When you forgive, you set yourself free*
- *Choose to be happy rather than be right*

Many people treat physical pain immediately because it hurts; they want a pain reliever or a surgery just to stop the hurt. But people carry wounds from emotional hurt for weeks, months and even years. They cling to the hurt that comes with pain, guilt, fault-finding, resentment and try to see for how much longer they can hold up. They don't know that they're subjecting themselves to emotional torture and hardship.

When you hold on to such feelings, you have given them your life; you've given them the pass to eat you up and control you. But if you control them and let them heal, it shows that you truly care about yourself. This is because clinging to the hurt from the past binds you in fetters. Forgiveness sets you free; it is putting your need to be happy before your need to feel justified. Rather than hold on to what someone has done to you, why not have a conversation with the person, stating your feelings and not necessarily heaving fault on the person? If the person who got on your nerves is not someone who matters to you, let it go. There are some ways to forgive more easily:

- See the person you need to forgive as someone who hurt you only because they didn't know of better ways to deal with their own insecurities.
- You have to realize that there is always an option or a choice when someone does something hurtful to you: you either let it eat you up or you let it go.
- Another path to forgiveness is choosing happiness rather justification.
- Look at it from this angle: What you think happened is actually not what happened.
- Go and expend all that negative energy on something. Hit your fists or a book. Throw something or scream until all the negative vibes are released.
- Treat the situation like it would become non-existent in the nearest future.
- Forgive and forget. Don't tie people to the impressions or "judgement" you have made of them based on what they have done to you. Concentrate on

their good behaviours and stop expecting them to mess up.
- As usual, love yourself.

Chapter 16: LOOSEN YOUR BONE, WILMA

Key Takeaways:

- *Have fun*
- *Loosen up, don't be too uptight*

Life in India reminds you to loosen up and not get cranky. Here are a few things learnt from a trip to India:

- Connect with people
- Have fun even when the unexpected happens
- Be the life of the party
- Know that when you have fun, you have not wasted your time
- Loosen up and be open to new things and as always
- Love yourself.

Chapter 17: IT'S SO EASY ONCE YOU FIGURE OUT IT ISN'T HARD

Key Takeaways:
- *Calm down and see the opportunities that abound around you*
- *Identify your excuses and do away with them*

Many people live life in a frenzy. Of course, people know what they want and try to work for it but stress themselves out in the process. We never take a pause to look at the situation and look for ways to get it done. People give themselves unnecessary tension because they feel like they cannot do anything because of their circumstances. It hinders you from fishing out the prospects and opportunities that abound around you.

Decide to release all the things you have attached to yourself that is not adding value to you. The way you perceive life determines your reality and you can change it once you change your mind set. The very way you run your life (living in a pile of excuses of why you can't do somethings) is a period to learn, stumble and get up but don't remain in that excuse-pile forever. Detach yourself from the negative vibes and reach out into what the world has to offer. To figure life out, make sure you act on the following:

- Know exactly what your excuses are. Identify the reasons you have negative vibes and poke the seeming logic in the "truths" you have come to accept and that you have gotten so used to.
- It's important that you figure out the negative outcomes that are attached to clinging to your truths. When the realization hits you, it is easier for you to release them and swap them for better amazing positive truths.
- Once you know what your current truths are as well as their outcomes, the next step is to dispose those truths.
- Make deliberate effort to start putting these things into practice. Concentrate on inculcating the positive habits. Get your groove on and make conscious leaping efforts to stay positive.
- Break your jinx and do something new. By doing that, new opportunities pop up and you can form new exciting truths.

- No matter what happens, avoid dwelling in self-pity and negative vibes. It's okay to feel sad but do not wallow in your own dirt.
- As always, love yourself.

Chapter 18: PROCRASTINATION, PERFECTION, AND A POLISH BEER GARDEN

Key Takeaways:
- *Delay is dangerous*
- *You'd never be perfectly ready for something, so just start anyway*

Sometimes, it's not just that you've never tried something but that you're afraid to do it. You expend strength on figuring out why you cannot do something. Why not channel that strength to do something productive? You're more knowledgeable than you think! Sometimes, go with the flow and be spontaneous; it makes things more exciting because when you keep getting "prepared", you may end up never doing it. Do what you have to, NOW. Procrastination is easier than actually doing what you have to do so rather than postpone, just do it.

These are some ways to stop delaying:

- Keep in mind that getting something done is better than waiting for the perfect time and resources. Just start out and you can perfect everything in the end.

- Take note of the times when you get tired or worn out during activities, so you can hand it over to someone else or figure out how you can maximize your peak period.
- Set a deadline with someone who will not pity you if you fault the deadline; someone who can discipline you or who talk sense into you. You could place a bet if that'll make you more answerable.
- If you realize that you work best under pressure, take your time and have fun and when time is closing in on you, work. If not, if you keep trying to work and your mind is not there, it will not work out.
- Please, again, love yourself.

Chapter 19: THE DRAMA OF OVERWHELM

Key Takeaways:
- *Have good time management habits*
- *Set your priorities right*
- *Make time your friend*
- *Don't kill yourself, take a breather when you need to*

Take things a step at a time. Don't drown in it and allow situations take their toll on you. We have many things to be grateful for. Crush the mindset that you have insufficient time to do what you want to do. There's always time for something you have prioritized as important.

To do this, revere time. Keeping to time and doing things in time keeps you in control of the time and helps you gain more time. If you keep treating time like trash, like it is not an important resource, you're going to lose out in the end. If you want time to treat you right, treat it right too. Start keeping to time- don't stand people up, follow your to-do list faithfully.

Next, identify the things that divert your attention and avoid them. Break big tasks into smaller bits so they become easier for you to manage and execute. Your brain can only take so much and overloading it will lead to under-productivity or work not properly done.

Don't always live with the idea that there are too many things you have to do so you do not have time for yourself. Quit emphasizing the fact that you have too many things to do. Rather, figure out what you love about these tasks and concentrate on them. See life from the perspective that you have responsibilities that your awesome self has to do and that you love these responsibilities.

Also, utilize your breaks to chill out and relax so you're mentally relaxed to continue with the tasks. Cherish the moments you get to stand up and walk around or even take a pee. You should also ask for another person's view on the task. You might have gotten so used to the task that you're stuck and can't see anything new. So get a fresh pair of eyes to look at it and suggest ideas or solutions to you.

Next, take a critical look at all the tasks you have to do and see how to make it better or how you can do it faster. Can you delegate some to other people? How can you make the task more interesting? Is it very compulsory you do all, at that particular time? With this, it is easier to prioritize and when you prioritize, you are able to know what to work on at a given time. It saves you stress. Another way is to hand it over to someone else to do for you. What are you not happy doing? What are you not very good at? What don't you have time to do? Look at all these things and if you cannot pay someone to do it, you can find other means of getting someone to do it.

Make sure you find time to rest and relax. Don't kill yourself, take a chill pill. To reduce regrets, take control of your time and design your life in such a way that you create time for yourself. Again, Love yourself, you deserve some accolades.

Chapter 20: FEAR IS FOR SUCKERS

Key Takeaways:
- *With fear, you have two options: let it eat you up or rise above it*
- *You don't have to always "play it safe"*

Fear is a choice. Fear, the big fat monster is always ready, seeking whom to devour. Once you allow it, it takes a huge hold of you. It clamps down on you and doesn't let you go so easily. But you have options: to let it hold you down or not.

There's a lot of inspirational talk about how you can do anything you set out to do but once someone wants to try and take a risk, we all shout, asking the person to play it safe. Below is a list of ways to deal with fear:

- Forecast the things you fear on a platform of triumph. View panic as a thing of the mind and it is easier to conquer.
- Get to the root of your fear and then turn it around to suit you. Change perspective and let your fear drive you to greatness. Use your fear as adrenaline.

- Channel your energy to maximize your innermost potentials. Don't give in to the panic because it's always worse in your mind than it is in reality.
- Be careful of what your mind feeds on. If you continually feed on fearful things, your mind will keep acting on them.
- If at all you want to stay up at night to think, be careful of where your mind wanders to. It is easier to get worked up about situations in the night because the hustle and bustle of the day is not there to distract you.
- As always, love yourself.

Chapter 21: MILLIONS OF MIRRORS

Key Takeaways:
- *Bits and pieces of yourself are in the people you associate with so if they bother you, check yourself*

- *Let go of people who drain you of positive energy; people who are toxic for you*
- *Learn to stand up for yourself*

When you meet new people, they often supply you with information about themselves. So, from your own standpoint as a person, you look at their totality and then decide if you want to know them more or not. Other people are like your reflectors. Your worldview is based on the realities that surround you as a person. Always try to learn from people's bad behaviours and not always act in response to them. It would help you grow as a person. The things that irritate you about other people are the things that affect you deep down and are most likely your insecurities and uncertainties.

When you come across someone that gets on your nerves, don't see yourself as victim of the person. Rather, face the issue and grow out of being a victim. This is because you eventually have to reconcile with the fact that you have your own shortcomings. If someone pisses you off and it does not resonate with you, you won't dwell so much on it but if it gets under your skin so much, it means you also need to check yourself about the issue you are complaining about. You catch the attention of people with the same behavior they see in you so when you have issues with someone, see what you can learn from it.

Make sure you always stand up for yourself when you can no longer deal with someone's crap, if not you'd be using that person to cover for your own unwillingness to stand up for yourself. Love yourself enough to stand by your beliefs. That way, you can catch the attention of like-minded people. You revere some people because they can stand up to anyone and are unapologetic about their beliefs. You revere them because they love themselves enough to not go down to anyone's level. Here are some ways to stand by your own truths without giving half a hoot:

- Identify the things that irritate you about others and them use them as reflections. Is it something that bothers you deep down? Or makes you anxious? Or you are trying to suppress?
- The next step is to poke around the things that get to you. Look at what that person is doing and then swap

it with you or your insecurities, so you can get to the root of the matter.

- When you discover that being around someone constantly drains you of all positive energy, leave them.
- If you notice that you've learnt from their terrible behaviours and have grown, but they still prefer to remain at their psycho level, don't get entangled with them anymore.
- It's not a cliché, love yourself.

Chapter 22: THE SWEET LIFE

Key Takeaways:
- *Show love now that you and your loved ones are still breathing*
- *Don't get too engrossed with life that you neglect those who care about you*

Do what you want to do now that you're young.

Show love to those you truly care about. Love them in spite of their silly attitudes and your differences.

Don't get too worked up that you forget or miss out on having fun with those who would always be there for you and those you can't do without.

Even if where you are not where you want to be, keep at it. Make yourself happy and have fun with yourself.

Love yourself now that you can.

Chapter 23: THE ALMIGHTY DECISION

Key Takeaways:
- *Stick to your guns when decide on something*
- *Desire it so much that you keep going no matter what happens*

When you take a serious step or make a serious decision, you have to stick by it no matter what happens. You have to remain stoic no matter what life throws at you. Some people think they've made a decision, but then quit when it gets uncomfortable. Truth is, they didn't make that decision; they only tried it out.

When you've decided to do something, you'll do all it takes to fulfill your aspirations. If you've only decided to try it out, then when you have to do something a bit difficult, you'd rather keep living your life the way you've been living it. You can do anything you truly set out to do and as they often say, "when there is a will, there is a way".

- Your desire for it must be so strong that you want it as bad as you want your breath.
- If you are indecisive, start training yourself to make decisions by starting to make small decisions as soon

as possible. If you are swift at making decisions, train your mind to think it through and then go ahead with it.

- Don't give excuses any chance to linger on or else you'll stall at what you want to do.
- Stick to your guns. Achieving your dreams is like being delivered of a baby. You conceive your idea and it begins to grow in you. You have to go through trimesters with their different challenges and then you begin to labor (the most painful) just before you birth your baby (idea). As your idea grows inside you, you get attached to it and you know you're pregnant of something beautiful. It's not going to be easy so be ready to get dirty. But no matter how many times you fall, pick yourself up and keep at it.
- Again, love yourself because you've made the decision to.

Chapter 24: MONEY, YOUR NEW BEST FRIEND

Key Takeaways:
- *Change your perspective about money*
- *Have a beautiful relationship with money*
- *Hang around people who have money or are at least, intently working towards having*
- *Be very specific with how you want your money to work for you*

Expand your worldview. Change your mind set. Broaden your horizon. You need to do all these if you don't want to keep thinking like a poor person. If you keep thinking you can't have a certain amount of money or you can't purchase certain things, you can never have them.

To receive the most of the money cycle, position yourself in a way to receive. Start operating like you're where you envision yourself and don't associate with people who only cry broke most of the time. Develop a beautiful relationship with money; tend to it and love it. Treat money right and it will treat you right. Don't make money inconsequential in your life. If you see money as something evil, it will never stay around you. Next, have a plan.

Stop concentrating on lack and start focusing on plenty supply. When you have the strong belief that you can have money, you exude good money vibes and you have aligned yourself in such a way that you can attract money's attention. When you decide that you want to live a small life, you do not only mess yourself up, you deny other people of the good things and awesomeness flowing from you.

Be honest about how you feel about money and note it. Now poke your current truths about money and flip it. Flaw all the logic in your truths about money and then create positive affirmations about it. "Confess" them and feel it resonate deep in your heart.

Next, know exactly what you need money for and the kind and amount of money you want. You need money for more things than the basic things. You need money to be the best version of yourself and share it with the world.

Money is very contextual; it is what we have attached to it that makes money what it is. It is the monetary value attached to an object that makes it what it is. It is what you believe that you will attract. When you demand money from your clients or ask for a certain amount of salary, you get the attention of people who already operate at that high level of energy. When you lower your own energy, you lower theirs too. Match your energy with your desired income. Keep pushing yourself to be worth the income you truly desire; acquire the skills and technical know-how. Associate with people who have high energy with money. Work hard to keep raising the energy that will attract money to you.

Read books that will up your awareness about wealth. Be friends with people who already have money or those who don't think it's bad. Have a good financial perspective.

Be around people who will propel you to be the best you can be by having the money you desire. Be around those who are better than you and can guide you on the path which you have chosen. Read about them, get to know them if you can and always be ready to learn. As always, love yourself and money will become your friend.

Chapter 25: REMEMBER TO SURRENDER

Key Takeaways:
- *Do your best and leave the rest*
- *Let go when you need to*

When you desperately want something and you go all about chasing after it and stressing about it, the negative vibes you exude keep pushing it away. It is not about sitting down and doing nothing, it is about doing your part and leaving the rest to fall in place by themselves. It is about relaxing your grip on somethings in such a way that you position yourself to let things come naturally to you. It is about having faith that as you are acting, the very thing you desire will definitely come. This is because when you get extremely desperate, you become ready to do anything to achieve your dream and covetousness and greediness sets in.

In as much as you try to take control of your life, let some things happen by themselves. It is a simple act of 'do your best and leave the rest'. Having faith and leaving the space for nature to take its course is surrender. It is like struggling when you're in water, you are sure to drown. When you release yourself, the water does its part. When you have envisioned your future, you sure do not know all the directions but you keep going.

Surrendering is staying open-minded to be able to recognize the right direction when it shows up. It is about staying true to what you want and letting nature guide you through it. It is about letting go knowing that you will still catch it. It is about waiting even while you are still acting. It is about being grateful that the life you so much desire will come.

Love yourself and the rest will fall into place.

Chapter 26: DOING VS. SPEWING

Key Takeaways:
- *You've heard enough, start acting*
- *Develop good habits*
- *Make like-minded friends and have a mentor*

You may have listened to several inspiring talks but when you eventually catch it and it sinks in, it's like a revelation suddenly dawns on you. The difference comes when "it moves from your brains to your bones". You sit up and then want to do something about your life. Some people spend years just living with the theory of having a better life and not actually doing anything about it. People who actually do amazing things continually break out of their comfort zones to stay amazing.

Once you start feeling like this is the best you can ever be, in no time you would go back to square one. Keep being better. Make sure your best days are never in the past. You have to keep learning, keep expanding, keep getting uncomfortable, and keep getting challenged. You never arrive because each new stage comes with its own fresh set of challenges. You have to keep evolving, keep breaking out. Keep doing something and let the Universe be your friend.

Discard the bad habits that have pushed your life to where it is now and swap them for good ones. Develop habits such as: time management, good decision making, good health practices, good money/spending habits and good relationship habits.

Take a breather when things are getting tough, and then act. Be friends with people who are achieving their goals and are living life the exact way they want it or at most are intent or doing so. It gives you a sense of wake up call to kick ass too. Set realistic goals, and break it into chunks. It's easier to move at your own tempo that way. Get a mentor because it will make your journey faster. They will keep you on your toes and keep you growing.

Align your body with your mind. Don't just laze around. Feel good about yourself. Talk sense to yourself and then start acting. Figure out what makes you happy or what keeps you pumped up with energy and do it often. Love yourself, with every fiber in your being.

Chapter 27: BEAM ME UP, SCOTTY

Key Takeaways:
- *Anything you want to do is possible*
- *Give positive vibes to attract positive vibes*

Have a strong belief that whatever you want to do in life is very possible.

Think "why not" instead of "why". Don't think you can't have what you desire because it won't end well or that it's too risky. Don't panic.

When you're happy with yourself and you do things that get you excited, you give off positive vibes and you attract positive vibes.

Know it deep within you that you can do anything you set out to do.

And you, yes you, love yourself, because you are amazing!

CPSIA information can be obtained
at www.ICGtesting.com
Printed in the USA
BVHW07s0809221018
530870BV00009B/1146/P

9 781718 041714